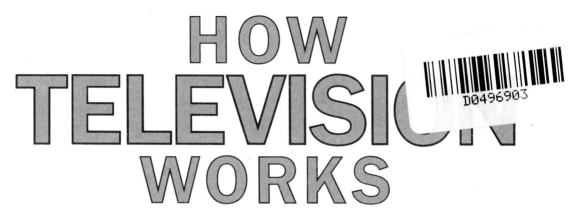

HOW TELEVISION WORKS

Written and designed by

Tony Potter and Robin Wright

Photographed by

Tony Potter

Consultant editors:

Judy Miles
Producer Schools Television

John Hawkins
BBC Engineering

CONTENTS

About this book

This book explains how television programmes are made. It takes you behind the scenes at a range of eight different programmes – from top soap opera *EastEnders* to Tony Hart's popular art and design programme *Hartbeat*.

Each programme has been chosen to show a different aspect of how programmes in general are made. Some, such as *The Chronicles of Narnia,* involve many people working over a long period to put together a series – in much the same way as a feature film is made. Other programmes, such as *Motormouth,* are broadcast live from the studio each week. But there is one thing that all programmes have in common – team work.

This book tries to give a flavour of how it feels to be a member of the team, either out on location with a film crew, or in the studio. To do this, it shows pictures of a typical day's filming or recording with each of the featured programmes.

Quite often, making programmes is a slow business. It often takes a whole day on location to film just four minutes of what you see in the end on the screen! Things are usually a bit quicker in the studio – about 12 minutes of drama can be recorded. This is because programmes are made with enormous attention to detail.

Throughout the book there are features on different aspects of programme-making. You can find out about everything from make-up and special effects to cameras and lighting.

Who's who

Some of the crew and cast in a scene from *The Chronicles of Narnia.*

The first part of this book explains who does what in a typical television programme. There can be a crew of as many as forty or fifty people, or as few as two or three.

How programmes are made

These two viewers were involved in writing an item for *Wildside.*

Whether it is a live show or a complex costume drama, all programmes follow a similar pattern – from planning, through script writing and rehearsals, to filming and editing to create the final video tape.

Broadcasting

Find out how programmes get from the television station to the set in your home on pages 44-47. Most viewers receive programmes broadcast from terrestrial, or ground-based, transmitters. Programmes are also distributed by satellite or cable links.

In this section you can also find out how transmitter or satellite signals are converted by your television into sound and pictures.

Programmes in this book

WILDSIDE

Wildside is a BBC environment programme with a difference – the edition on tropical rain forests featured in this book was presented by two children – in a supermarket in Avon! Find out more on pages 8-11.

Prince Caspian

The Voyage of the Dawn Treader is the second of CS Lewis' *Chronicles of Narnia* to be filmed by the BBC. It features a host of extraordinary creatures and some spectacular special effects. Find out more on pages 12-17.

EastEnders

The BBC's *EastEnders* is recorded 50 weeks of the year on a film studio "lot" which recreates a slice of London's East End. Four complete production teams are needed to keep up a tough schedule. Find out more on pages 18-23.

Palace Hill

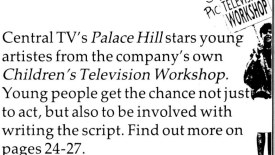

Central TV's *Palace Hill* stars young artistes from the company's own *Children's Television Workshop.* Young people get the chance not just to act, but also to be involved with writing the script. Find out more on pages 24-27.

News at One

John Suchet, presenter of ITN's *News at One*.

Presenting a news programme is a hair-raising business. Imagine going on air not knowing exactly what was going to be included in the programme. Find out more on pages 28-31.

Sports Science

Film cameraman lining up Judy Leden, Ladies' World Hang-Gliding champion, in a shot.

BBC Schools Television made this series of programmes about science in sport. Filming from a hang-glider presents plenty of technical problems. Find out more on pages 32-35.

Motormouth

Neil Buchanan, Tony Gregory and Gaby Roslin, the presenters of Motormouth.

Motormouth is one of TVS' top children's programmes, networked to other ITV regions live on Saturday morning.

Hartbeat

Hartbeat, the BBC's long-running art and design series gets a staggering 56,000 pieces of work sent in by viewers each series!

Tony Hart and Margot Wilson with two young viewers who visited a recording of the programme.

Who's who

These two pages describe the jobs of a typical television crew and explain what each person has to do. It is essential that everyone works as a team – all programmes are the result of a team effort.

The production team

There are usually about nine key people involved in the production team. Each plays an important part in the production process. Sometimes, several jobs are done by the same person.

The producer
The producer is in charge of the overall "look" of a programme, or the "house style" if it is a series. He or she is often responsible for a strand of programmes.

The director
Responsible for the creative side of a programme and keeping to the budget. He or she decides on camera shots (for example, close-up, pan, or track) and angles; also what the programme looks and sounds like.

Production assistant (P.A.)
Indispensible to the director. She does all the organising, office work and types scripts. She also lists and times each shot. In the studio she calls shot numbers out to the "floor".

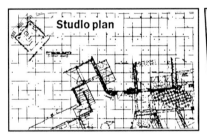

Designer
The designer designs and plans the set, or any locations, working closely with the director. She or he must be an expert on construction and leave space for the cameras to move about the set.

Production unit manager (P.U.M.)
The "trouble shooter", who also finds suitable locations. They arrange hotel accommodation and organise facilities, such as Portaloos, if they are needed on location.

Floor manager
They are the link between the studio floor and the director in the control room who instructs them through "cans". The floor manager relays the director's instructions and cues the cast to start and stop.

Assistant floor manager (A.F.M.)
Responsible for the care and maintenance of props and for ordering any that are needed. Another important job is to mark up the studio floor at rehearsals according to the designer's plan.

Researchers
Responsible for tracking down any background material needed for a programme, such as historical details, film clips, photographs, good questions for quiz games and facts about specific topics.

Writers
Writers make commentaries and scripts for presenters and news readers. Writers often work closely with video editors, matching the story with the pictures.

Technical team

There are many technical people involved in the production of a television programme, without whose skills and expertise few programmes would ever reach the screen. These people are trained to operate complex equipment or create items such as scenery.

The camera operators
They take their instructions from the director through "cans" or from signs by the floor manager. A card clipped on to the side of the camera gives them the details of shots which are needed for each scene.

Sound engineers
They sit up in the sound gallery, above the studio floor, next to the control gallery. They control all the sound from the studio floor and mix in music, or other required sound effects.

Lighting engineer
He or she controls the lighting on the set, giving the effect which is needed for the scene being shot. Instructions are also given to electricians on the studio floor to move lights when necessary.

Vision mixer
In the control gallery the vision mixer sits at a console with over a hundred buttons on it. The buttons change the pictures on the monitors from one camera to another as required by the director.

Special effects and props
Many programmes use special effects, such as revolving images. Props (short for "properties") are all the objects used in scenes.

Dubbing mixer
Dubbing mixers put sound effects on to edited films, such as voices on animated cartoons. The dubbing suite has a screen and a control console by which sounds and vision are matched precisely.

Video editor
After the programme has been recorded on video tape, the video editor cuts, splices and even re-arranges sequences. This is done according to the director's instructions on an Assembly Order.

Make-up artists
They must have a detailed knowledge of how the strong studio lighting affects appearances, and what make-up is needed. Make-up artists also make wigs and other items to alter a person's appearance.

Wardrobe supervisors
These are responsible for either making, buying, hiring, repairing and cleaning the numerous costumes which may be needed for programmes. Costumes may have to be altered to fit an actor or actress.

How programmes are made

Most television programmes are made in similar stages, from the idea through to the time when they appear on your television screen. Once an idea has been approved, a script is written. Next there is a meeting between the director, producer, production assistant, and the designer. The budget is carefully planned, and rehearsals are scheduled.

The director meets with the producer and designer. The budget and rehearsals are planned.

Facilities
The facilities include arrangements such as hotel bookings or other accommodation. On location, vans for changing, make-up and portaloos may also be required.

Locations
The production unit manager will book studios and arrange for the locations requested by the designer, obtaining permission for the production unit to film there.

Design
The designer plans and is involved in the construction of sets, such as the one above which was used for the BBC's production of Narnia. A studio floor plan is also drawn.

Rehearsals
The production assistant has typed the script, and the director plans shots with help of the floor plan. It takes about three days of camera rehearsals to film and record a one and a half hour programme.

Special effects
Any special effects which are required are organised by the special effects supervisor. Dry ice makes smoke or fog.

Shooting the scenes

The cameras follow the shooting schedule, which gives information about the type of shot required: CU (close-up), MLS (medium long shot), MS (mid-shot), MCU (medium close-up), BCU (big close-up). The floor manager relays the director's instructions.

The director, the production assistant and vision mixer sit up in the control gallery, separate from the studio floor. They can see what is happening on video monitors. The PA cues the cameras, and the director talks to the FM through her 'cans'.

Post production

After all the scenes have been shot, the video tapes, or film have to be edited. The director and producer watch a rough edit, from which they work out a final assembly order. Finally, the title music and credits are dubbed on to the film or tape.

The video editor uses an electronic editor to edit the tapes. He may use up to three machines.

The director watches the preliminary edit of a film. These are called 'rushes'.

The final stage: music and credits are dubbed on to the final edit.

Film editing

The director views the rushes with the editor. The rushes are then spliced together according to the assembly order. A cutting negative is made from the final edit.

Programme schedules

All that remains to be done is to plan when the programme is to be shown. This partly depends on the type of audience, and what other programmes are being shown.

Wildside

Wildside was a magazine series for children, covering wildlife and environmental stories. It was shot on location, with children as the presenters. Conservation of wildlife and the environment were the main concerns of the programmes, which also suggested ways in which viewers might help preserve the natural world.

Letters from viewers

The series follows on from *The Really Wild Show*, and came about as a result of letters from viewers. One viewer, Flora Maitland, wrote in expressing her concern about the destruction of the Amazonian rain forest.

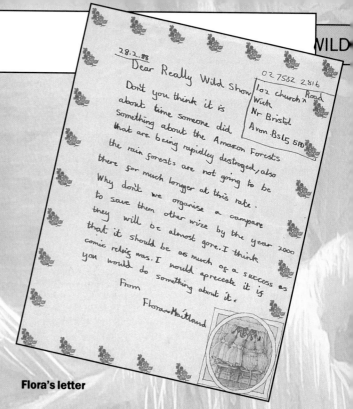

28.2.88

Dear Really Wild Show

02 7582 2816
102 church x Road
Wick
Nr Bristol
Avon Bsl5 5RD

Don't you think it is about time someone did something about the Amazon Forests that are being rapidley destroyed, also the rain forests are not going to be there for much longer at this rate. Why don't we organise a campare to save them other wize by the year 2000 they will be almost gone. I think that it should be as much of a success as comic relieg was. I would appreciate it is you would do something about it.

From

Flora Maitland

Flora's letter

Programme idea

When the producer of Wildside read Flora's letter, it gave her an idea. Because Flora had already made the connection between many of the products in this country and their place of origin, it was decided to shoot the item on the rain forest in locations such as a supermarket, a Do-It-Yourself shop, and a sweet shop.

Programme content

Each of the Wildside programmes were 25 minutes long, with six or seven items of about four minutes each. Flora and her younger brother, Luke were given four to five minutes on air to say what they felt about the destruction of the rain forests.

Mahogany

Fruit

Here are some of the products which either come from, or have ingredients from the rain forests.

Supermarkets such as Sainsbury's are becoming more aware of their environmental responsiblities and label their products accordingly.

ENVIRONMENT FRIENDLY

Planning

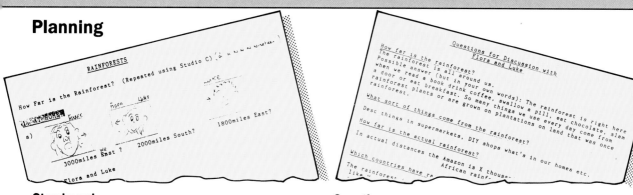

Storyboard
The producer works out a story board for each location, with sketches showing what each shot should look like and how they are linked.

Questions
A list of questions for an "interview" with Flora and Luke has been drawn up. This is for additional voice-over material.

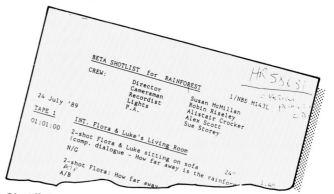

Shooting script
This lists all the scenes in each location which are to be taken, and the sequence in which they are to be shot.

Shot list
The production assistant lists all the shots during the filming. She then produces this list, giving the time of each. This makes editing much easier.

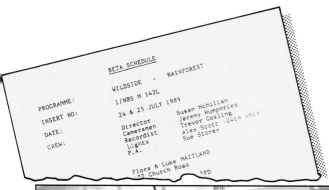

Shooting schedule
A copy of the shooting schedule is sent to everyone involved in the filming, including Flora and Luke, to let them know where to be and when. Everything is now ready for filming the next day.

SHOOTING SCHEDULE
Morning

The crew set up outside Sainsbury's supermarket. Flora and Luke were pushing trollies around for test shots. A boom mike was used to catch the background noise of cars.

Filming starts inside the store. Flora and Luke head straight for the fruit section to search for products from the rain forest.

Shot of Luke at the vegetable shelves talking about rain forest products. He is fitted with a radio mike to cut out background noise.

Flora and Luke approach with their baskets full of rain forest products. The producer asks the cameraman to take a shot of them at the checkout.

Afternoon

Location: W.H.Smith's Do It All store. Close-up of Luke among the plants, as if in a rain forest. This pans out to show that he is in a DIY store.

A shot of Luke framed in a toilet seat. He talks to camera about the origin of the wood.

The producer wants a shot of Luke knocking on a door, as if he is trying to find out if the wood comes from a rain forest.

Flora full face to camera in the kitchen section of the store. She points out that a lot of furniture is made from rain forest wood.

The camera man holds the camera low, to get a shot of Flora and Luke standing at the wood stacks.

Voice-overs

After shooting the scenes, the sound engineer records some voice-overs. These are needed as there was not enough information about rain forests during the filming.

Running order

The final video tape will be edited down to four or five minutes. The item on rain forests is one of seven in this edition of Wildside. The producer then has to decide on the actual running order for the programme.

Prince Caspian

The *Voyage of the Dawn Treader* is the second of CS Lewis' *The Chronicles of Narnia* to be dramatised by Alan Seymour for the BBC. Six half-hour episodes were filmed by director Alex Kirby, in much the same way as a full-length feature film. A cast and crew of about 120 people were on location in Wales, the West Country and the Scilly Isles for three months during the summer of 1989. During this time the crew had just three days to catch up if the film slipped behind schedule, so work carried on regardless of the weather.

Alex Kirby directing a scene.

The Dawn Treader

The Dawn Treader is a central part of the story, and production designer Alan Spalding had to find a boat to match the programme's Victorian romantic medieval style. He worked closely with the director, costume designer and boat builder to adapt an old Breton crabber. The boat had just a flat deck, which made it easier to design a structure which could be bolted on top. After the sailing sequences had been filmed, the structure was unbolted and used in studio scenes.

Dawn Treader

The dragon's scales were made from carved and painted polystyrene.

The crows nest and rigging were based on a late medieval boat.

The figurehead was made from fibreglass by a sculptor.

Planning

Every scene in a drama has to be carefully planned months before filming begins. Work on *Prince Caspian* began over 18 months before the programme was transmitted.

First the producer commissioned the script writer. Then the director was engaged once a first draft of the script was written. Alex Kirby's first job was to visualise how he wanted the film to look, bearing in mind the budget for the series.

Storyboards

The director works with a designer to produce storyboards, which are small drawings of every scene. They are used to work out how the script should be treated visually, and to see how the film will look overall.

A storyboard.

Production team

The director employs all the people needed to produce the film. One of the first members of the team was the production designer, Alan Spalding. Alan's job was to make sure that all the visuals for the film would look right. Alan and his team had to find five locations for the filming, organise the ship and set building and buy or make all the props.

Artistes

The director holds auditions to select the cast. Most of the central characters of *Prince Caspian* are children. There were also many animal parts for small people, such as the part of *Reepicheep*. Most of the artistes are booked through agencies.

▲ **Warwick Davis as *Reepicheep*.**

Tutor-chaperones

Children of school age have to have lessons while they are filming during term time. A tutor-chaperone is engaged to look after the children and to teach them during breaks in filming and in the evenings.

◀ **Sophie Wilcox and Richard Dempsey.**

Make-up

It took over twelve weeks to plan the make-up for this programme. Sylvia Thornton, the make-up designer, and her team had about 40 wigs and beards to create, along with nine animal heads and shoulders and 21 noses and ears. The team work from a caravan while on location.

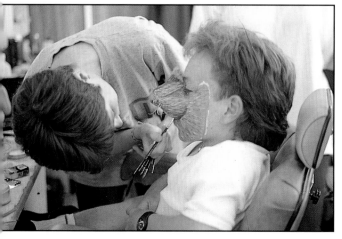

A make-up artist applying the finishing touches to *Reepicheep's* face (Warwick Davis). It takes over an hour to apply.

The make-up artists have to repair their work during the course of the day.

Sylvia Thornton working on Sophie Wilcox. Sylvia decides on the style of make-up with the director and the costume designer months before filming begins.

Costumes

The costume designer based her costumes on medieval dress. The team includes two assistant costume designers and three dressers. The dressers help the artistes into their costumes and take care of them when they are finished. Dirty costumes are washed at the end of each day in the costume caravan. The dressers make sure that the same things are worn for different "takes" of the same scene.

Catering

A crew on location take everything they need with them – including a mobile canteen.

Some of the crew and cast at breakfast before filming begins.

Camera

This programme was recorded on videotape rather than film. Film is more expensive than video. Here, the cameraman is discussing with the director how he would like a shot.

Sound

This picture shows one of the sound recordists sitting in the *Dawn Treader's* cabin, out of camera shot. You can also see him in the picture below.

Narnia was shot using a single camera, unlike in a studio where several cameras are used. A simple dialogue between two characters involves first filming one person's lines, then moving the camera to film the other person. The two parts are later edited to look like a continuous conversation.

The sound crew included three sound recordists and two boom operators. The sound is linked directly to the camera, so that sound and pictures marry together, or synchronise, perfectly. The programme was recorded in stereo, making it very difficult to get rid of background noise, such as passing jets.

The camera is mounted on a "Spyder" so that it can be moved smoothly along rails.

One of the boom operators.

Stunt man

A stunt man was needed for one scene to double for *Prince Caspian*. The stunt was quite simple – diving from the side of the ship. The stunt man was carefully chosen to be of a similar build to *Prince Caspian* and dressed in an identical costume and wig.

Safety divers were used to pick up the stunt man from the icy water as soon as the dive was filmed.

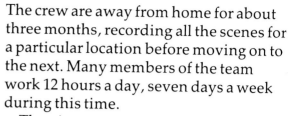

Loading supplies on board the *Avon Adventurer*, one of the support vessels. The AFM, Sue Stuart, checks that everything is OK.

The *Dawn Treader* comes in view at the rendezvous point.

The crew are away from home for about three months, recording all the scenes for a particular location before moving on to the next. Many members of the team work 12 hours a day, seven days a week during this time.

The pictures on these two pages were taken of scenes being recorded for episodes 2 and 3, on location off the coast of Wales, near Milford Haven. Two support vessels were used to transport the crew and supplies out to sea to rendezvous with the *Dawn Treader*.

The support boats were also used as floating platforms for the camera to film scenes on board the *Dawn Treader*. This meant transferring the heavy equipment from one boat to another each time a change was needed.

The director rehearses the cast for the first take of the day. He checks the camera positions and runs through the lines. The technical crew prepare equipment for use later in the day.

A swell causes the boat sides to rub together and squeak during the first take of scene 403. You can see the cast and crew trying to hold the boats apart long enough to shoot the scene.

On to the next shot on the starboard side of the boat. The Production Unit Manager, Mick Evans listens on his earphones to check that everyone is ready before the shot starts.

Running repairs

Minor damage to the boat is repaired on the spot. Carpenters quickly repair the damage and repaint the timber to match the original colour.

Make-up and costumes are constantly checked and adjusted to make sure everything looks the same from shot to shot.

Lunch arrives! Everything stops for a few minutes. Easily eaten food is brought for artistes playing parts with complex face make-up, so that they can eat without damaging the make-up.

Make-up designer Sylvia Thornton makes the boys' legs look suntanned, ready for the next scene.

A make-up artist adjusts the stunt man's wig.

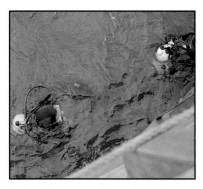

Safety divers stand-by, while the cast on deck rehearse a scene where the children are to be made to look as though they have just been dragged out of the water.

The children are soaked to make it look as though they have been in the sea.

Camera trouble! A problem with the camera means that the wet cast have to be wrapped to keep them warm while the fault is fixed.

Finally, the camera is repaired and everyone starts again. This scene will be at the beginning of episode 3. Two actors appear to pull the children on board, while the divers wait below.

The boom operator and cameraman get sound and pictures as quickly as possible. The safety divers are below the children in case anything goes wrong.

Last of all, the children are put in the sea from a rubber dinghy. The safety divers help them into the water. The shot will end episode 2, where they will appear to have been dropped in the sea.

EastEnders

The soap opera *EastEnders* is watched by millions of people on Tuesdays and Thursdays each week. In order to make the half-hour episodes, four complete production teams are needed, fifty weeks of the year. There is a cast of around 25 regular artistes, two dogs and many extras who appear in the background. The team only get two weeks holiday at Christmas by doubling the number of recordings at some other time during the year!

Filming a scene off Albert Square.

Each episode is made up of scenes filmed in the programme's 20 indoor sets, or outdoor scenes filmed in the "lot" – a re-creation of a slice of London's East End.

The script

John Maynard, *EastEnder's* script editor works with three or four writers to produce plots and scripts, nine months ahead. He directs the plot and chooses stories and "cliffhangers" which he wants to feature. He and his team write a script timed exactly to fit the episodes.

Rehearsals

Every scene has to be rehearsed in the rehearsal room with one of the four directors. He gives the cast directions on where they should stand, how they should move and deliver the lines, anticipating where he will place the cameras. Complex scenes are rehearsed several times. Rehearsals are timed with a stopwatch in case any adjustments need to be made to the script.

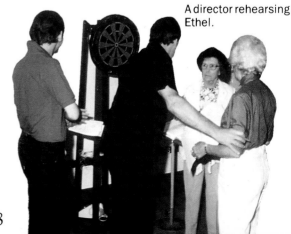

A director rehearsing Ethel.

The "Vic" is made from plywood.

The production crew set up the market stalls on the lot each day.

The lot

Albert Square, the "Vic" pub, cafe, laundrette and other buildings are all in the "lot". The lot was built in 1984 under the direction of designer Keith Harris.

All the buildings are constructed of plywood over a steel frame, with plaster "bricks", in what was waste ground at one of the BBC's studios. Their interiors are all sets in the studio. It took eight months to design and build and was a real gamble at the beginning – no one knew that *EastEnders* was going to be such a success! Buildings are still being added.

Lighting

Scenes are recorded on the lot eight weeks behind transmission and two weeks ahead of studio recordings. This means that the lighting and weather conditions filmed outdoors can later be matched in the studio.

Lights being adjusted ready for recording.

Props

All the props are made to look convincing on camera.

One of the few lot buildings with an interior is the shop. Like everything else in *EastEnders,* all the props have to be changed from time to time to look up to date.

19

The cast

Members of the cast each have a dressing room at the studios, and rooms where they can meet to learn lines, reply to viewers' letters or simply pass the time between scenes.

The script for each episode is available about a week before recording and the lines have to be learnt by heart.

Gretchen Franklin, who plays the part of Ethel, reckons that soaps are "the toughest job in television". She thought her role in *EastEnders* was the hardest work she had done in 50 years' acting.

Gretchen Franklin (Ethel) with her screen companion, Willy.

Producer and director

The producer has overall control of the dramatic content and style of the programme, while the director rehearses the actors, devises camera positions and works out how to create what the producer wants.

Corinne Hollingworth, the associate producer, views the recordings made on the lot from a caravan. She gives precise instructions to the director about how she wants things to go.

Director Darrol Blake rehearses a scene. He has just a few days from script to shoot and 300-400 shots per episode to record in the studio and on the lot, so speed is essential. He views the unedited tapes at home.

Make-up

There are three members of the make-up team: a make-up designer and two make-up artists. Care has to be paid to making sure that the continuity is right – this means checking to see that each artiste's hair and face look the same from one episode to the next. This is especially important on *EastEnders,* as scenes shot on the lot are not completed in the studio until two weeks later.

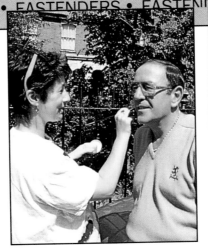

Mike Reid's make-up is adjusted on the lot.

Make-up designer Benita and her assistant fake highlights in an artiste's hair for a hairdressing scene.

Polaroid snaps are taken to help check the make-up continuity.

Extras

Many extras are used in *EastEnders,* to give the impression of busy London scenes. Children often get parts as extras, as they are needed to create a realistic effect.

Lot van

All the usual gallery facilities are crammed into a van on the lot. The PA times the shots, takes notes on good takes and communicates with the floor manager. The vision mixer cuts between cameras according to the script. The sound supervisor checks sound levels and runs the tapes.

The lot van.

Inside the lot van.

Animals

Animals, such as Willy, have their own dressing room and handler. Willy is hired through a theatrical animal agency. The handler makes sure that Willy is fed, exercised and behaves!

And action!…

The pictures on these two pages show some of the scenes shot on a typical day on the *EastEnders* lot. The lot is made to look like a typical London market by "dressing" it, with vans, cars, fresh fruit and vegetables, rubbish and so on. Each day the rubbish is swept away and packed into dustbin bags ready for use again. The lot has its own milk float and even a double-decker bus. There is a bus garage too – in reality the back of the scenery stores with a London Transport symbol fixed to the roof!

Getting ready

Work on dressing the set begins at 7.00am on lot days. Lighting, camera and sound crews also make an early start.

The camera crew assemble a track for a "Spyder". The camera is mounted on this and slid along.

The lighting crew assemble their equipment according to plans worked out in advance.

08.30 already. One of the AFM's and a designer discuss final ideas for dressing the lot.

Pick-up shots

The director needs a pick-up shot – one which will later be edited into the beginning of another sequence. Arthur is to run out of the phone box.

Allotment scene

Dot and Chris are having an argument in the allotment. The filming takes a little time, as reflectors are adjusted. These are used to reflect natural sunlight on to the scene instead of using electric lights.

Market scene

Various shots of the market scene are taken. The props crew and designers have to make sure that there is enough rubbish in view of the camera to make the scene look convincing. The floor manager and her assistants cue the extras to walk across the scene at the right time. Several takes are needed, as passing aircraft cause too much background noise.

Frank's car lot

To prepare for filming a scene at the car lot, the camera crew tape pieces of paper over the cameras. This prevents the bright sunshine from reflecting on the camera filters.

Garden scene

Pauline (Wendy Richards) is filmed sitting in the garden through an open door. This will later be edited to fit material recorded on the indoor set of her house.

The director gives instructions on how he wants Frank (Mike Reid) to react to news brought to him at the car lot.

Palace Hill

Palace Hill is a comedy series with a touch of political satire. It takes up to ten months to make, from the written ideas to the finished tapes. Production starts in mid-June and all episodes are complete by September or October. There are six episodes in the series, the first of which is transmitted about three months after production has finished. The cast consists entirely of children and young people who are members of the Junior Television Workshop.

Locations and ideas

The episodes for the show are shot in various outside locations all over the midlands. Many of the ideas for the show come from the members of the Junior Television Workshop who are involved throughout the production.

A promotional leaflet for the Junior Television Workshop.

Junior Television Workshop

Central Television's Junior Workshop was set up in 1983. It consists of a pool of over 200 young actors from Birmingham and Nottingham, aged between 7 and 19. Workshop members are involved in a wide range of drama, including courses on improvisation and technique.

On location for one of the scenes, with Binky Spoon (Gail Kemp) on the bike, and Nick Knuckle (Oliver Hawker) being made-up on the ground.

Auditions and rehearsals

Auditions are held with groups of about 30 students and children from the Workshop. The director looks for individual talent, taking into account people's ability to work in groups.

During rehearsals, the director briefs the cast for each scene. It takes about 10 days to rehearse for two days filming in the studio, and a whole day in the studio to record seven minutes of edited film.

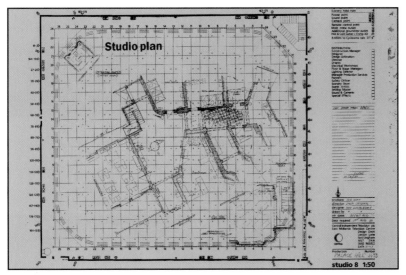

Studio

Several sets for different scenes and episodes are constructed in the studio, allowing enough space for the cameras to move round each one. Episodes and scenes are not shot in sequence. Instead they are shot according to the set involved. For instance, all the classroom or submarine scenes are shot together.

Boom camera

Boom cameras mounted on trollies are used for taking overhead shots on the various sets. The camera is attached to a boom which can be extended, retracted, raised, or lowered.

In the studio

The director consults the script, then briefs the actors in preparation for shooting the classroom scene.

The sound engineers are ready in their control room. Levels from the studio floor are checked ready for filming.

After briefing the actors for a scene, the director and his assistants direct filming from the control room.

The producer watches all the filming on a television monitor so that she can see what it will look like for viewers.

Special effects

"Exploding sherbet" is needed for one scene. This is made with foam. Air from electric fans makes it bubble.

A process called chromakey can make actors look as if they are flying. They are first filmed against a blue background.

This is a circular special effects lens. It can be used to make actors appear to revolve or turn upside down.

A classroom scene for episode 4. It will be filmed through the window.

Bossy Maggie (Tessa Harrison) and the cast wait for the director's signal.

Wardrobe assistants help the actors into their costumes.

There will be several takes for each scene being filmed for the episodes. This is why it takes so long to make a recording of just a few minutes.

Once the director is satisfied with the takes, the final recordings will be edited into the correct episodes. This is done when all the episodes have been filmed.

A snow scene. The snow is made from polystyrene granules.

Studio scenes, like the ones above and opposite, are constructed from wood and canvas to look as realistic as possible. Below you can see how the inside of the submarine was filmed.

News At One

Both major networks, BBC and ITN transmit up to four news programmes daily. Over six million viewers watch the lunch time television news each day. ITN's share of the audience ratings is just over two million. Audience ratings for news depend as much on what type of programme follows, rather than the content of the news itself.

The networks have journalists and correspondents stationed in the major cities all over the world.

Mobile film units can record events as they happen, to give up to-the-minute news.

Telephone and satellite links allow news to be transmitted from one side of the globe to another.

Television news

The medium of television affects the presentation of news. Unlike printed news in papers, television is an active medium which can bring viewers news stories as they actually happen. Newspapers can only deal with an event after it has happened. A television news programme is being made right up to the time it goes out on air. This requires close cooperation and split-second timing between all the members of the news production team, both inside and outside the studio.

The news team

Like any other television programme, a complete production team is needed to make News at One. The production team includes the news editor, presenter, writers, VTR editors, researchers, make-up, camera, sound and lighting crews.

Andrew Tilling, the senior news editor discusses stories with John Suchet, presenter and associate editor. The editor has to look ahead to see which stories are likely to develop and break.

The VTR editors edit video tapes of stories so that they run to a specific time and fit into the programme.

Feature and script writers often work with VTR editors so that pictures and commentaries fit together properly.

The news desk and television cameras are in the studio. Studio lighting is set by the computer.

The links between various news items in the programme, both inside and outside the studio, are coordinated from the central control room. The items are shown on screens and can be cued into the programme at the appropriate times.

The commentary scripts are fed into a central computer and transferred to an autoscript. This is a machine which shows the script in large print a few lines at a time, but is invisible to viewers. The presenter reads the autoscript text for each story.

Morning

Senior news editor, Andrew Tilling reviews the stories for today's programme. News at One runs for 25 minutes. The news editor has to decide on the running order for stories, and how much time should be allocated to each one.

John Suchet, the presenter, checks through the papers carefully every morning for any stories or developments which may need to be included in the programme. He is an associate editor, and takes part in the editorial decisions.

Meeting with the senior editorial team in the news room. The final running order and time allocation to each story is decided upon. Also, how each story is to be presented must be discussed: should there be film, or stills with voice-overs?

Throughout the morning, writers are working on stories and features. Feature writers work with VTR editors, who assemble film and video pictures to match the commentary, or voice over.

Checks for any live interviews or reports from overseas or locally.

Checking the running order with any stills which have to be used.

A team of writers prepares the scripts for the stories.

Afternoon

Less than an hour to go. John Suchet has a final run through the stories with the writers. He will make a last check of reports coming in from around the world.

The presenter is made up. The bright studio lights can make people's faces look shiny, so a little powder is used to take the shine off.

A final look at the scripts and running order whilst being wired up for sound. All those appearing in the programme are fitted with tie or collar microphones.

John Suchet gives a brief taster of today's programme from the news room.

In the studio the camera crews are ready. A final adjustment to John Suchet's microphone.

Towards the final count down: In the control room the producer and production assistant stand by. The vision mixer waits for the signal to start rolling the opening captions.

Stand by news desk! Two minutes to go. A last adjustment to the presenter's microphone as he chats with a guest he will be interviewing for one of the stories.

The team relaxes with a sigh of relief after the successful completion of the programme. As one Head of Operations put it: "…We make it with seconds to spare most days".

31

Sports Science

Sports science is a unit of five 20-minute programmes for secondary schools. The aim is to present sport in an interesting and new light by introducing the audience to some of the research being done to help athletes improve their performance. The emphasis is on sport rather than science.

Judy Leden, Ladies' World Hang-Gliding Champion.

Champion Hang-Glider

Judy Leden is the Ladies' World Hang-Gliding champion. She worked for several days with the Sports Science team, demonstrating techniques and equipment.

Director and producer, Judith Miles.

Production assistant, Jennie White.

Cameraman, John Beck.

The production team

This is a relatively small production team, with the producer doubling as director. The cameraman offers advice about shots and also tries to anticipate what the director wants. Great care has to be taken with sound recording, since weather conditions can affect the quality. A camera is attached to the hang-glider, and there are also sound links to the ground.

Assistant cameraman, Andrew Murray.

Sound recordist, Les Honess.

Special facilities, Peter Harris.

Technical requirements.

A film, rather than video camera will be used because different lenses are needed. A remote controlled camera will be attached to the glider.

The film camera can take different types of lenses, such as telephoto, or wide angled, which are needed for filming this project.

This "gun camera" is fixed to the hang-glider to film Judy Leden as she is flying. She can operate it by

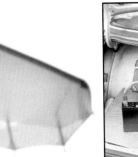 

On the left is the walkie talkie unit which is being used by the sound recordist, above, to direct the hang-glider.

The microphone has to be shielded with a fabric cover. This breaks up and reduces wind eddies and so produces clearer sounds.

The tape recorder uses a tape which has electronic pulses on it. This helps the sound and pictures to be matched later, during editing.

Making the programme

The location was high up on the Sussex downs. Filming was dependent on weather conditions: too little wind, or too much would make hang-gliding impossible. The team had to be prepared to film an inside sporting activity somewhere else with an alternative day for hang-gliding.

Morning

Judy Leden

The production crew meet at 10.00 and begin to unpack their gear. Judy Leden is ready with her hang-glider.

The crew assembled ready for filming on the South Downs.

The series of pictures below show the crew filming Judy as she takes off in her hang-glider.

Stand by to start filming.

Ready: Action!

John Beck, the cameraman attaches the automatic, remote controlled camera to the hang-glider.

Special facilities technician, Peter Harris, connects up the remote control switch.

The sound recordist, Les Honess, wires Judy up with a microphone for her link with the ground crew.

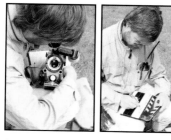

Andrew Murray prepares the camera. After he has done this he marks up the clapper board.

The lenses have to be cleaned regularly. An amber filter is used for filming into the sky.

Les Honess puts tape into the recorder. On the right, Judy Leden waits for the filming to start.

Afternoon

During the afternoon, Judy will be filmed taking off and flying over the downs. The director's instructions are relayed by the sound recordist, who communicates by walkie-talkie. Judy's own comments are relayed back through her sound link.

Cameras rolling.

Lift off!

Andrew Murray stands by with the clapper board, as John Beck prepares for a shot of Judy.

The director, Judith Miles, discusses some of the shots she wants with the cameraman.

Filming the hang-glider over the downs. The sound recordist (right) is giving instructions to Judy.

The production assistant, Jennie White, records the shots, and times each one with a stop watch.

The director wants a last shot of Judy talking about her hang-gliding equipment.

Filming Judy as she packs away the hang-glider and the rest of her gear into the bag.

Motormouth

Motormouth is a magazine programme for children. It goes out live on Saturday mornings before a studio audience. The programme includes cartoons, quiz games, interviews with bands and pop stars; also live reports on various topics and sport.

The presenters
Gaby Roslin on the right, Tony Gregory in the middle, and Neil Buchanan on the left.

Making the programme

The three presenters meet on Wednesday afternoons to go through the items they will cover on Saturday's show. On Thursday they meet with Motormouth's team of researchers to make sure that they have accurate information for the items. Rehearsals take place on Fridays.

Schedules
These are information sheets giving the times for rehearsals, transmissions and breaks. They are sent to everyone involved in the show.

Call times
A list of call times is sent to each member of the team, telling them exactly what time they are needed on the set.

The production team

There are usually about 22 people involved in the production of Motormouth. These include the director and producers, with their assistants; cameramen, sound engineers, floor managers, lighting technicians, designers, make-up and wardrobe people. The production is controlled by the director, who gives radio instructions to the floor manager in the studio.

```
MOTOR  UTH : SERIES II (SHOW 2 )  :    TECHNICAL RUNNING ORDER...
PROD N. :  K15 MO9                      ON AIR:   09.25.02
TXN DATE  : SATURDAY 16TH SEPT 89
                                        R/T:      01.49.48
PRESENTERS ; NEIL BUCHANAN/TONY
GREGORY/GABY ROSLIN/STEVE JOHNSON       3 X CB'S:    11.40

                                        OFF AIR:  11.26.30
```

ITEM/CONTENT	SET	SOURCE	CAMERAS	SOUND	R/T
1. CHILDRENS ITV IDENT		VTR A		VTR A	1.00
edited to: TEASER (IT'S MM 2 & IT'S TORTURE/JASON D QUASAR/BATMAN) edited to: TITLES					
2. INTRO'S	MOUTH	LIVE	1,2,3	STUDIO	0.45
Neil/Tony/Gaby & audience kids with ycyos. Steve in BG threatening					

Running order
The production team have copies of the running order for the items in the programme. Each item has to be very carefully timed to fit into the show, which lasts two hours. The running order sheets also give information about the sets, cameras and sound.

Floor manager and assistants

Studio floor
The floor manager passes on the director's instructions to all those working in the studio. She and her two assistants make sure that everything in the studio runs smoothly during filming.

Camera

Lighting
The lighting director, console operator, and vision engineer control the lighting. Between them they synchronise the lights to get the effects needed in the studio. The lighting for each set is programmed by computer.

Sound gallery
Here, the sound supervisor and gramophone operator control all the studio sounds. The supervisor decides on the type of microphones and where each should be placed. All the sounds from the studio can be adjusted to get the effects needed in the studio.

The control gallery
From here the director and his assistant communicate with the floor manager by a radio mike. Next to them are the producer and musical associate. The vision mixer and effects mixer are in charge of the stills and special effects that appear throughout the show. The production team sit in front of television monitors which allow them to see what is going on in the studio.

Rehearsals

Rehearsals for the show take place on the Friday and on the Saturday morning before the programme is transmitted. Rehearsals are especially important, because Motormouth is a live show. It is essential that each item in the show is timed exactly, so that the programme does not overrun and interfere with the programme schedule for the rest of the day.

The audience arrives by coach.

The audience

There is an audience of 32 children for the show. They are picked up by coach from a different region each week.

It's Torture

This is the name of the show's main quiz game. The audience is divided into four teams of eight, so that everyone gets a chance to play the game. Each person has to answer a question. A wrong answer means being pushed closer to the edge of a sludge pit. A correct answer results in someone in the other team getting pushed nearer.

The studio is prepared for the rehearsal. Lighting, sound are checked. Stage hands put up the set. The floor manager, her assistants, and cameramen are ready.

Steve Johnson is the game show host. He gets to know the audience before the show, and briefs each team before the programme. All his questions are set by the programme's researchers.

Dry ice is used to make a smoke effect. It is kept in a metal container. When air is mixed with it, it gives off a dense vapour which looks like gas or steam rising from the "sludge" pit.

Saturday

Final rehearsals for the show take place on Saturday morning between 0815 and 0915. The set, lighting, and cameras are prepared at 0700. The presenters are on call at 0730.

The camera has a copy of the running order for the cameraman to follow.

The floor manager directs the cameraman, while filming a sketch.

After the rehearsal is over, a final lighting check is made.

The sound supervisor and his team make a final sound check to the studio floor. All the radio mikes and sound levels are checked.

Everyone on the studio floor is ready for the show to start. The audience and presenters are in their places.

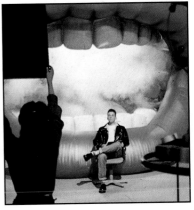

Tony Gregory starts the show.

Final count-down

The director instructs everyone on the studio floor to stand by. The vision mixer and effects mixer have checked their screens to see that everything is working properly. The show's titles come up on the screens, pre-recorded on one of the studio VTRs. The director's assistant counts... 9,8,7,6,5,4,3,2,1...Action!

Hartbeat

Hartbeat is a long running and successful series of art and design programmes presented by Tony Hart. It developed from the well known 1960s programme for deaf children, called Vision On. The idea of the programme is to help viewers extend their creative skills. There have been over 100 editions of Hartbeat since it began eight years ago, recorded at the BBC's Bristol studios. Each week the programme has a different theme.

Tony Hart, and one of his assistants, Margot Wilson. During the 25 minute programme they demonstrate different drawing, painting and design techniques for viewers.

Behind the scenes

The backdrop for the set of Hartbeat. This is painted on to a cloth drape which hangs outside the wooden windows at the back of the set.

Here you can clearly see the folds in the cloth backdrop. When the programme is being recorded, the backdrop looks completely realistic.

Another view of the painted scenery and wooden windows. The bush adds to the realistic effect.

Behind the scenes: a view of the patio doors, showing how they are constructed. Note the lighting on the left.

The set has been created to look like an art studio. You can see how real the back drop looks through the windows and patio.

Setting the scene

The producer, Christopher Tandy, and his assistant, Amanda Gabbitas. Chris Tandy's aim is to make the 25 minute programme visually interesting, so that it stimulates viewer's interests. Each week he and his assistants sort through around 56,000 items sent in by viewers. They try to choose something which will go with the theme of that week's programme.

The special effects specialist, Peter Harwood, and Martin Peplar, the film editor, (on the left).

They work in the dubbing studio, matching sounds to film, video and animated drawings for the programme.

Three cameras are used in the studio. On the left is the boom camera with its two man crew. All three cameras are moved round the studio to get the shots the producer wants.

The studio: the three cameras can be clearly seen. The boom camera is mainly used for bird's eye shots of Tony or Margot working at the desk. Here Tony is discussing what is required for the next shot with Cliff White, the floor manager.

Filming the programme

Tony Hart and Margot Wilson choose some of the paintings which have been sent in for this week's show. The cameras film the paintings as Tony and Margot discuss them.

Getting made up

Both the presenters are made up for the programme. Make-up is necessary in a television studio as the lights are very bright and make people's faces look shiny.

Getting steamed up

The theme for this week's show is 'North'. Tony introduces this by saying that the radiators are cold. He hits the pipes to unblock them.

The radiator pipes "explode", covering Tony with steam. The "steam" is made by a smoke cannister in a machine which blows the smoke out.

Margot's model of the North Sea oil rig.

One of Margot's ideas for the theme is a North Sea oil rig. She shows viewers how to make a model.

In the control room Margot can be seen constructing her model of the oil rig.

The producer explains how he wants to film Tony making a drawing for them of the 'North'.

Tony begins his drawing. He is using felt-tip pens and chalk on paper. The boom camera films him from overhead.

Tony's completed drawing of the 'Terra Nova'. He has used the drawing to demonstrate the dramatic effect which can be achieved by using felt-tip pens and chalk.

Tony Hart ends the programme by thanking viewers for all the work they have sent in.

HART BEAT

Hartbeat
BBC Television
LONDON W3 6XZ

Broadcasting

There are several methods of transmitting television programmes to the millions of television sets in Britain. Cable links are expensive and only viable in densely populated urban areas. Satellites are also expensive and they only have a limited life of ten years in space. The main method of transmission in Britain is by radio waves.

Transmitting the programme

There is a network of 50 high-power transmitting stations in Britain, which transmit television pictures in the form of Ultra High Frequency (UHF) radio waves. Each station transmits four programmes: BBC1, BBC2, ITV and Channel Four. The network is continually extended, with a new transmitting station being opened every two weeks.

A map showing the main high-power transmitters in the UK.

The transmitting station

The video signal from the studio is only strong enough to provide a picture for one screen. At the transmitting station the signal is boosted by a high-power transmitter. It is then converted into Ultra High Frequency (UHF) radio waves, and transmitted from aerials up to 300 metres high.

Relay stations

Hundreds of low power relay stations form part of the transmission network. Signals from the high power transmitter are picked up by a high quality receiver, then relayed further along the network. Though a signal may be relayed several times, its quality on the television screen is still very high.

Satellite links

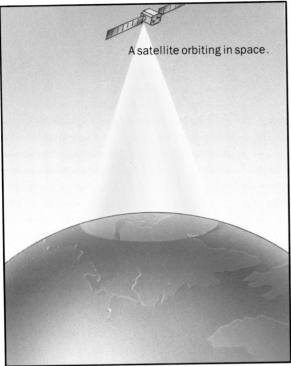

A satellite "footprint" map.

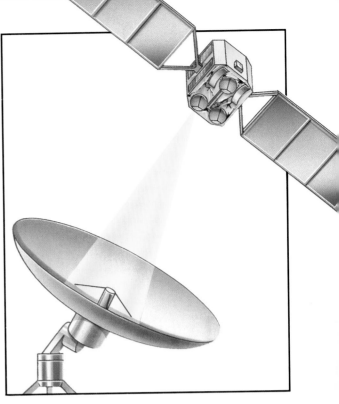

The large dish aerial which sends the signal to the satellite.

The dish aerial

A large dish aerial is used to send a concentrated beam of signals to the satellite. The dish is automatically steered so that it is always pointing to within 0.1 degree of the satellite.

The satellite receives the signals on one set of channels, converts them to another set and transmits them back to earth again.

The presentation suite

The last link in the transmission network is the Presentation Suite. Here the presentation editor introduces the programme before it is routed to the appropriate channel.

Malcolm Eynon announcing a programme.

How the programme reaches the screen

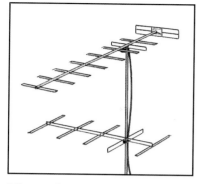

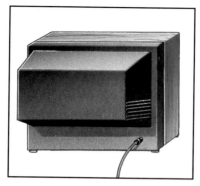

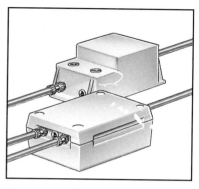

The radio signals from the transmitter can be picked up by a VHF receiving aerial mounted on the roof of a building.

A single cable from the aerial is fed down from the roof. This is connected to the back of the set.

In areas where reception is not good, an aerial amplifier may be needed. In a few cases a relay system may be required.

Satellite reception

To receive transmissions from a satellite, a small dish aerial has to be installed, pointing directly at the satellite.
The television set amplifies the signals from the satellite. There is an extra tuner which selects the required channel.

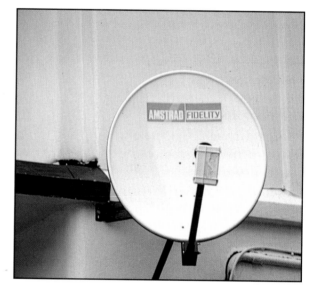

Cable television

Cable is used where reception is very difficult, such as a mountainous area. Modern cables use optical
fibres which can carry many channels at once. Cables are buried and linked to houses from distribution boxes.

Inside the television set

Signals come from the aerial as tiny electrical voltages, only a fraction of the power of a torch battery.

Inside the set, the tuner picks out the signal which the viewer has selected for watching a chosen programme.

There are two signals for each channel: sound and vision. Each is carried on an Ultra High Frequency radio wave.

Signals and voltage

Vision and sound are electronically separated, or demodulated, from their carrier waves to make them visible on the screen. The video signal is a voltage which varies with the brightness of the scene shot by the camera. Variations in the brightness trigger red, green and blue beams, "telling" them what colours to make the picture. If you look carefully at the screen, you can see the three coloured stripes.

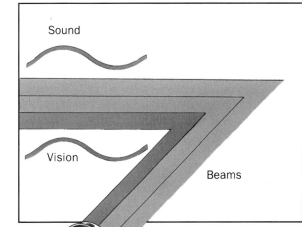

Scanning

The picture tube, or cathode ray tube, cannot read the whole picture at once. Instead, the picture is "read" by electronic scanners 25 times a second until it is built up on the screen. The scanners are synchronised with the camera by pulses, to reproduce what it sees.

Cathode tube

The three colour beams are projected onto the cathode tube to colour the picture when it is scanned.

Painting

Pictures are painted in lines. It takes 1/25 of a second to build up a complete picture.

Index

Paperback ISBN: 0 563 34578 0   Hardback ISBN: 0 563 34579 0

Origination by RCS Graphics Ltd
Typeset by Etel Computer Setting
Printed in Britain by BPCC Paulton Books Limited

The publishers would like to thank the producers, directors,
crews and casts of all the BBC and ITV programmes featured in
this book for their invaluable advice and support.

Additional picture credits
p7 (bottom left) Luke Finn **p18** Chris Gilbert **p19** (top and
bottom left) Chris Gilbert **p20** Chris Gilbert **p21** (centre right
and bottom left) Chris Gilbert **p22** Chris Gilbert **p23** Chris
Gilbert **p24** Central Television **p44** BBC Engineering **p4-5** (top)
Guy Smith (bottom) Luke Finn **p46** (top) Guy Smith (bottom)
ZEFA **p47** Guy Smith